5
Solutions
To
Save America

Douglas V. Gibbs

ISBN: 1979649006
ISBN-13: 9781979649001

To those who understand that without action, liberty cannot be preserved – and that action without the proper knowledge is nothing more than an opportunity to spin one's wheels.

DOUGLAS V. GIBBS

• Note to Reader

There will be times, while reading this book, you will come across "united States." In these instances, the lack of capitalization of "united" is purposeful. When the Declaration of Independence was constructed, the union of States were not officially the "United States of America," yet. Recognizing the Colonies were independent and sovereign "states," but that the union was not yet one that comprised a national entity, the opening lines of that document leaves the word "united" not capitalized. We must also remember that at the time the country was being brought together into a new union, the attitude was not the "United States Is" (a single nationalistic entity as we view it today, and a designation essentially in place since the War Between the States). The people of the Founding Era viewed the new country as the "United States Are," a pluralistic collection of sovereign States united together for the purpose of establishing greater strength and unity. The States ratified the U.S. Constitution with the understanding that the new federal government would protect, preserve and promote the concept that the union was populated by States who remained sovereign, autonomous, and in control of their local issues. During the early years of the existence of the United States of America, citizens of this great land did not view themselves as Americans, but as citizens of their States. They were Virginians, New Yorkers, Pennsylvanians, and so forth. The preservation of the concepts of sovereignty and autonomy of the States were of utmost importance. The concept of localism, where the States handled their own internal issues, and any central government would be only given authorities to handle external issues and issues necessary for making the union more perfect, was a necessary part of what the American System was all about, and a crucial ingredient in the recipe that makes this country a "republic", and not a "democracy". Part of our dilemma in today's political atmosphere is the fact that State Sovereignty, and the autonomy of the States, has been reduced greatly. In today's environment of a rapidly expanding central government the federal government is increasingly encroaching on internal issues in a manner never originally intended. It is the responsibility and obligation of We the People to address the problem, and establish a strategy to combat it.

• Setting the Table

The federal government was created to serve the States, and We the People; not to rule over them.

According to James Madison in Federalist Paper #45, "The powers delegated by the proposed Constitution to the federal government are few and defined. Those which are to remain in the State governments are numerous and indefinite. The former will be exercised principally on external objects, as war, peace, negotiation, and foreign commerce; with which last the power of taxation will, for the most part, be connected. The powers reserved to the several States will extend to all the objects which, in the ordinary course of affairs, concern the lives, liberties, and properties of the people, and the internal order, improvement, and prosperity of the State. The operations of the federal government will be most extensive and important in times of war and danger; those of the State governments, in times of peace and security."

The United States Constitution is a social contract between the States to create a federal government to serve them in the capacity of handling issues the States either could not, or should not, handle while participating in a union of states that comprises a national entity.

For the delegates of the States who wrote the U.S.

Constitution, the key was to find a balance between forming a successful country with a strong central government, yet restraining that central government in such a way that the rights of the States as constituents in the new country were also preserved.

The Constitution was written in such a way that, as a contract, it expressly enumerates any authorities the federal government may have. It was not designed to be interpreted, or for additional unlisted powers to be implied. Like a contract, either the authority is plainly listed in the Constitution, or it is not. If the power is not expressly enumerated, or necessary and proper in order to carry out an expressly enumerated power, the federal government does not possess the authority to carry out said power.

Unfortunately, the federal court system has established over the last two hundred years a complex web of case law that is used to twist and usurp the Constitution at the whim of judges who support various political agendas. The power of the courts to "interpret" the Constitution has become accepted by all layers of government, by those who are involved in the practice of law, and by the general public. The power was gifted to the courts, supporters of *judicial review* will tell you, by the courts themselves. John Marshall's opinion of the *Marbury v. Madison* case in 1803 is normally the source of the authority for such a power, according to most legal academics.

The power of *judicial review*, which equates out to be an allowance for the courts to be the final arbiters of the U.S. Constitution, does not exist in the actual text of the document, and therefore the power does not technically exist from a constitutional viewpoint. However, the courts claim to posses, and be able to wield the power, nonetheless. As a result, a structure of case law now haunts our American System, and is often used as a source of authority for federal actions, and modifications in federal powers.

If a person simply reasons out the unconstitutional implications of *judicial review*, it should not take long for the individual to realize that the alleged power of the courts to determine the constitutionality of the laws they review presents a monumentally consequential deviation from the Constitution the alleged power truly poses.

The U.S. Constitution was written to create a federal government limited in its scope and powers, providing only authorities enabling the new federal system to handle external issues, or issues that directly influence protecting, preserving, or promoting the union of States (such as the postal service, mediating conflicts between the States, or establishing uniform standards regarding our currency, or system of weights and measures). The federal government, with its limitations as provided by the U.S. Constitution, may only gain any additional authorities with the permission of at least three-quarters of the States approving such a request through the amendment process. The States, after all, hold *original authority* over all issues and all authorities. The States are the parents over the federal government, and the federal government exists at the pleasure of the States so as to serve the States.

The federal court system's claim of possessing the authority of *judicial review* (The court's perceived ability to determine if a law is constitutional or not) also unconstitutionally provides the ability to strike-down any law deemed as being unconstitutional based on the opinion of a judge, or group of judges. In the case of federal laws, this means that the federal courts, which are a part of the federal government, may determine if a federal law is constitutional or not (in other words, determine if the federal government has authority over the power in question in the federal law in question).

What is happening, then, is that the federal government, through the federal court system, is determining for itself what its own authorities are. How is that a limited government as originally intended by the Founding Fathers?

Article I, Section 1 of the United States Constitution reads, "All legislative Powers herein granted shall be vested in a Congress of the United States, which shall consist of a Senate and House of Representatives."

From the point of view of the original intent of the United States Constitution, the power to make law, modify law, and repeal (strike down) law belongs solely to the legislative branch.

In our modern political environment, however, what has been happening is that the judicial branch has been acting legislatively through *judicial review*, and a large number of Presidents have been acting legislatively through their issuance of executive orders.* What we have, as a result, is an American System that bears little resemblance of the original system put into place when the Constitution was written in 1787, and ratified in 1788. Therefore, it is our job to begin the work to return our system back to its original form.

"The good sense of the people will always be found to be the best army. They may be led astray for a moment, but will soon correct themselves."
~ Thomas Jefferson

* Executive Orders are constitutional. George Washington's Thanksgiving Proclamation was an executive order. However, executive orders are not legally allowed to carry any force of law. Executive orders are supposed to only be either proclamations, or instructions delegated down to the departments of the executive branch for the purpose of executing the laws of the United States.

• Opening Salvo

When the English Colonists reached a point of "enough is enough," originally the American Colonists did not violently revolt. In the beginning, they protested and rallied. The resulting violent revolution was neither planned, nor was it a preferred method of change. In the end, however, a bloody revolution turned out to be the only solution remaining in the quiver of the colonist's bundle of strategies for independence. After the violence broke out, and the Revolutionary War was escalating, to make the separation from Mother England official, delegates from the colonies wrote the Declaration of Independence. In that document, not only was a list of grievances enumerated in it, but also a set of opening paragraphs explaining why the separation of the political bands with the British Empire was not only desired, but necessary.

As Englishmen, the Colonists recognized that they had Natural Rights that gave them "separate and equal station to which the Laws of Nature and of Nature's God entitle[d] them." Their possession of Natural Rights, which included the right to "alter or to abolish" the government under which they were governed, were "self-evident" to them as a virtuous people. They recognized that God created man and endowed humanity with "certain unalienable rights" before *government by men* ever existed.

The message to King George was clear. The Crown, and the members of Parliament, were breaching the social contract they had with the English Colonies, and the leadership of the British Empire was violating Natural Law. In order to be able to freely pursue "Life, Liberty, and the pursuit of Happiness," a new government was needed to replace the tyrannical one that was at that time working to force the English Colonies into submission and compliance with "repeated injuries and usurpations." To create a new government, the "absolute Tyranny" over the States would need to be dissolved.

The English Colonies appealed to the King of England, hoping to appease the monarchy and parliament into granting to the colonists fair and equitable treatment. The calls for fairness were rejected by King George, and answered with an increase in the number of British Troops stationed on the Atlantic Shore of the New World. The confrontations became more violent, and finally shots were fired, launching the English Colonies and the British Empire into a War for American Independence.

A little more than a year after the "Shot Heard 'Round the World" on April 19, 1775 in Lexington, Massachusetts, delegates from the States put forth in July of 1776 a Declaration of Independence, transforming the colonies into a union of sovereign States. The delegates capped the famous document with a unifying, courageous, and telling pronouncement; "And for the support of this Declaration, with a firm reliance on the protection of divine Providence, we mutually pledge to each other our Lives, our Fortunes and our sacred Honor."

> **"What a glorious morning is this!" ~ Samuel Adams, after hearing news of the Battles of Lexington and Concord.**

In the eyes of the British Government, the signers of the Declaration of Independence were traitors. Their treason would be prosecuted, swore the monarchy. All 56 signers of the document would suffer, in the long run. Some lost wealth, property, or the lives of family members. Some were imprisoned, and some lost their lives themselves during the war. All of them, however, were prepared to give that ultimate sacrifice, "writing a check" as we say about our military veterans, "up to and including their lives for the purchase of the freedom of people they never met, and many who were yet to be born (Posterity)."

A little more than a decade later, after the end of the war, and the formation of a new country no longer under British Rule, delegates from the States met again in Philadelphia, in the same room of the same building that the Declaration of Independence had been debated, to construct a new document. During the Summer of 1787, for slightly longer than four months, people we refer to as our Founding Fathers met again, some of them the same people who debated the Declaration, and some of them new delegates there to represent their States, but this time to write a new constitution to fix, and ultimately replace, the Articles of Confederation.

The Articles of Confederation had been written and signed during wartime. It was a wartime document designed to help further unite the new united States who were in a war with the British Empire. During the first few years of independence, however, it was realized that the government under the Articles was too weak. Shays' Rebellion, an internal uprising by the veterans of the American Revolutionary War, revealed the weakness of the confederate government. As a result of being unable to pay their creditors with the worthless money issued to them by the new government as compensation for their service in the military struggle against Great Britain, veterans of The Revolution staged an insurrection that included them blocking the front steps and entryways of court houses to keep their creditors from filing against them in the court of law.

While the weak government under the Articles was unable to do something about the insurrection, the merchants of Boston were willing to use their collective wealth and power to take action. Massachusetts Governor James Bowdoin and the Boston merchants hired and mobilized a force of 1,200 hired guns to engage the veterans of the Revolutionary War, bringing the confrontation to a violent and bloody end.

In the Preamble of the United States Constitution it reads, "We the People of the United States, in Order to form a more perfect Union, establish Justice, insure domestic Tranquility, provide for the common defence, promote the general Welfare, and **secure the Blessings of Liberty to ourselves and our Posterity**, do ordain and establish this Constitution for the United States of America."

In the line that reads "secure the Blessings of Liberty to ourselves and our Posterity," the founders did a curious thing. The word "ourselves" begins with a lower-case "o". Posterity is capitalized.

While nearly all of the nouns in the Constitution are capitalized, words were also often capitalized to show emphasis. In the case of the line in question, *emphasis* was the reason behind the capitalization of the word "Posterity."

The line reveals a lot about the selflessness of the Founding Fathers. They were explaining to us in that line of the Preamble of the United States Constitution that, yes, they were doing all of what they were doing, including, but not limited to, the creation of the Constitution, for their own opportunity to enjoy the Blessings of Liberty, but they were especially doing it for their Posterity. . . their capital "P" Posterity – or should we say, "those not yet born."

While we, as Americans, endeavor to restore the

republic, and save America from those who oppose the principles and philosophies contained on the pages of the Declaration of Independence and the United States Constitution, we must realize that the Founding Fathers serve as our example. Yes, we wish to save America for our own freedom and liberty. But, in truth, our duty and obligation to resist evil and protect liberty goes beyond ourselves. We must engage the enemies of liberty not only for ourselves, but for our Posterity. For our children. For our grandchildren. And, for all of those generations not yet born.

• Solution #1: Revolution

The world has seen revolution many times throughout history. Only once did the outcome of a bloody revolution result in liberty, rather than tyranny. The differences between all of the violent revolutions in history, and the one launched in America in 1775, were only two things. The American Revolutionaries fought for individualism, and did so with a firm reliance on the protection of divine Providence. All of the other revolutions, the failed revolutions that resulted in the rise of tyranny, were all about collectivism, and godlessness.

Karl Marx wrote, "Communists everywhere support every revolutionary movement against the existing social and political order of things. The Communists disdain to conceal their views and aims. They openly declare that their ends can be attained only by the forcible overthrow of all existing social conditions. Let the ruling classes tremble at a Communistic revolution. The proletarians have nothing to lose but their chains…Working Men of All Countries, Unite!"

If ever there was a movement that was reminiscent of the mood of the original American revolutionaries who brought about the independence movement in the American Colonies over two hundred years ago, the Tea Party that emerged during the rise of Barack Obama is it. Inspired by the desire to oppose a tyrant, and defend the choice words of patriots, both movements led to great changes. The big difference is that those who fought for independence during the American Revolution had to achieve their goals through a bloody revolution. In 2008, American patriots faced off with what they believed to be the rise of a potential tyranny, but the confrontation was waged through a peaceful revolution.

On February 19, 2009, Rick Santelli's rant on CNBC inspired the already rising movement. Santelli made remarks about the Homeowners Affordability and Stability Plan, accusing the government of bad behavior, and suggested that the people should revolt in the form of a Tea Party. His call for a Tea Party was answered by cheers, whistles, and applause. The video went viral, and subsequent rallies emerged in various cities, dubbed Tea Parties. Many believe the peaceable Tea Party assemblies drew their inspiration from Santelli's rant. Santelli's words of common sense fanned the flames of a movement, one that already had in mind what it was going to do, but it needed just the kind of the nudge that Santelli gave it.

When the Tea Party movement first emerged on the scene in 2008, during the presidential campaign season, many Americans flocked to the small local patriotic rallies. People knew in their gut that something was wrong as the opponents of the U.S. Constitution tightened their grip on the American form of government. As Americans, we knew that the liberal left's newfound stranglehold on America was dangerous, as was their latest presidential candidate, Barack Hussein Obama. However, we failed to understand exactly how to combat the leftist attack on our freedoms. Patriots moved on the symptoms while initiating a revolt against the establishment leadership in the Republican Party, but the smooth talking Democrat Party presidential candidate had already caught the hope and imaginations of a whole slew of uninformed voters.

The Tea Party Movement began what became a peaceful revolution, and in truth, a counter-revolution against a coup against the American System of Government. The hard left Democrats held Congress and the White House together for only a short time, however. In 2010 the voters gave the House of Representatives to the Republican Party. In 2014 the Senate was also delivered electorally to the GOP. Then, during a campaign the media had proclaimed belonged to Hillary Clinton, the voters provided for the seemingly unlikely victory of the Donald J. Trump for President Campaign in 2016.

Over 240 years ago the American Revolution began as a peaceful revolution. The colonists rallied and protested, not realizing that their revolution would become a violent revolution in the end. John Adams, during that time period, wrote, "The Revolution was effected before the War commenced. The Revolution was in the minds and hearts of the people."

The founders did not expect to go to war. They had hoped the differences between the King and the colonies could be settled peacefully. The King, however, had other plans.

> **Jefferson wrote to George Washington in 1796: "One loves to possess arms, though they hope never to have occasion for them."**

The reasoning of the English Colonists that a peaceful revolution could change their system of governance back to one of liberty was heavily influenced upon the fact that such a revolution had occurred once before in history. In 1688, in Britain, The *Glorious Revolution* changed the path of British History, leading to the flight of the king, and to the English Declaration of Rights in 1689. During The Glorious Revolution a shot was never fired. The revolution had been carried out by peaceful means.

As we have seen, the influence of the Tea Party on elections has been powerful. The candidacy and election of Donald J. Trump as President of the United States was a direct result of a conservative movement established and nurtured by the Tea Party.

In the beginning, the Tea Party revolution began with rallies and protests; massive gatherings like the one occurring in Washington D.C. on September 12, 2009, christened the "Taxpayer March on Washington". Then, as the politicians began to squirm, the Tea Party transformed into a political movement, forming a Tea Party Caucus in Washington, and at a number of State Capitals. Other groups emerged, or regained momentum they once had enjoyed. Conservative and Republican Clubs emerged and flourished around the country. The anti-constitutional forces of government were no longer being tolerated. The message of a peaceful revolution was effective, and spurned change in government that was revolutionary, and virtuous. Liberal Left forces, however, like the Redcoats of

> **"A little matter will move a party, but it must be something great that moves a nation."**
> **~ Thomas Paine, Rights of Man, 1792**

King George's British Army, have not been willing to work with the Tea Party and conservative uprisings. As we saw during the era of the birth of the United States, the statists are meeting the peaceful revolution offered by those who desire to return the republic to the principles of *laissez faire* with violence. This time, however, it's not the Redcoats, but Marxist backed agitators who call themselves names like Black Lives Matter, La Raza, and Antifa.

> **Laissez Faire** - A policy or attitude of letting things take their own course, without interfering. Abstention by governments from interfering in the workings of the free market.

During the Obama presidency, it crossed the minds of many patriots that perhaps it would be necessary to storm the White House and forcefully remove the Usurper in Chief, but that's not the way conservatives normally fight the good fight. Besides, in this age of technology and hair-trigger stress, the move would have been both dangerous and irresponsible. We are a republic, not a democracy, which means this is not a nation governed by mob rule. It is our responsibility to affect government through our representatives, and the various methods and processes authorized by the U.S. Constitution. While the strategy of using constitutional philosophies to move forward our peaceful revolution seems slow and time consuming, we must not let our impatience lead us to the taking up of arms, and the use of violence, against the offending members of the U.S. Government. As we saw in the 2016 Election, if we can mobilize the patriots of this country, blood in the streets is not necessary to bring about revolution. A redirectionary kick of the government into the right constitutional direction can be achieved through advocacy, and the tactics given to us by the Founding Fathers when it comes to keeping the republic.

We must also understand that revolutions don't begin nationally. They begin locally. The best way to engage change at the federal level is to get our local governance under control. Change always begins with the proper local corrections.

Washington is full of cockroaches, but where did the

infestation begin? What good is complaining about the cockroach infestation in Washington if we are breeding them locally?

While our right to bear arms is predicated on the concept that if the federal government should become tyrannical we the people should be able to take it back by force, that kind of violent reaction by conservatives and constitutionalists is exactly what the liberal left is hoping for. Every time there is a violent mass shooting, they hope and pray (to *whom* they pray presents a whole different conversation) that the shooter is some crazed right-wing, gun-toting, Bible-thumping conservative. The reality is that none of the modern mass shooters have been Republicans, conservative, or NRA members.

> **The National Rifle Association (NRA) is the oldest civil rights organization in the United States; established in 1871 to provide rifle marksmanship training. Early on the NRA got involved in protecting the gun rights of the newly emancipated slaves so that they could defend themselves against the Democrats and Ku Klux Klan. The KKK was created for the sole purpose of acting as the militant arm of the Democrat Party, using violence to keep blacks from voting.**

If a civilian militant operation was launched against the federal government the leftist members of the federal government would use it is an excuse to clamp down harder, make the voices of the States and Congress even more irrelevant, and tighten controls over our gun rights. Then, the hand of the people would be forced, and a violent conflict would ensue. That is what is behind the emergence of groups like Black Lives Matter, and Antifa. They are like the bully in the schoolyard poking us in the chest, trying to get a reaction. The problem is, the moment we take a violent swing at them, it will serve as an excuse for their own bloody reaction, which would serve as a call to government to quell the violence in the name of establishing "peace and safety."

This is not to say that violent revolution is always a possibility in the game of restoring liberty, and keeping the republic, but as the American

> **For when they shall say, Peace and safety; then sudden destruction cometh upon them, as travail upon a woman with child; and they shall not escape. ~ 1 Thessalonians 5:3**

Revolutionaries discovered, it can be a real possibility if the statists demand it.

As indicated earlier, The American Revolution was not originally intended to be a war. The colonists hoped to come to a peaceful understanding with Britain, before taking military action. However, they also recognized the reality that bloodshed may be necessary. While the early drive for independence remained fairly non-violent, in the end the determination of the revolutionaries, and the refusal of the British to yield any ground, led the conflict towards a military confrontation.

War, while not preferred by the colonists, became a reality when the British came for the guns and ammunition of the colonists in Concord, and were stopped short by a militia at Lexington Green. Even then, bloodshed was not intended by the colonists, but began when a single shot rang out, and the itching fingers of the British infantry pulled their triggers in response.

Thomas Jefferson, after the creation of the federal government by the U.S. Constitution in 1787, remarked that a revolution may be necessary once every twenty years. In fact, he so distrusted the formation of a central government that he stated, "God forbid we should ever be twenty years without such a rebellion. The people cannot be all, and always, well informed. The part which is wrong will be discontented, in proportion to the importance of the facts they misconceive. If they remain quiet under such misconceptions, it is lethargy, the forerunner of death to the public liberty. ... And what country can preserve its liberties, if its rulers are not warned from time to time, that this people preserve the spirit of resistance? Let them take arms. The remedy is to set them right as to the facts, pardon and pacify them. What signify a few lives lost in a century or two? The tree of liberty must be refreshed from time to time, with the blood of patriots and tyrants. It is its natural manure." ~ Thomas Jefferson, November 13, 1787, letter to William S.

Smith, quoted in Padover's Jefferson On Democracy, ed., 1939

Jefferson was not encouraging bloody revolution, but he was recognizing the potential tyranny of government, and the possible need for bloody revolution in order to neutralize the rise of tyranny.

Hence, the reasoning behind the insertion of the Second Amendment into the U.S. Constitution, via the Bill of Rights. I am a firm believer that the primary reason for the existence of the Second Amendment is to enable the populace to take up arms against the government, if necessary. Imagine how different history would be if the Germans had taken arms against Hitler before he confiscated their guns?

During the Russian Revolution, and the French Revolution, in an attempt to shed the shackles of tyranny, the people found themselves enslaved by a whole new kind of authoritarian madness. An armed revolution too early can be just as devastating as one carried out too late.

Knowing that a violent revolution should be our last resort, through the Constitution the Founding Fathers gave us other tools specifically designed to enable a restoration of our constitutional legacy. They recognized the importance of the will of the people, but like every other part of our system, decided to divide the power of the people, too.

While we have democratic processes in our system, we are not a democracy. The United States is a republic, and republics require more involvement by the citizenry than a "vote once per year and be done with it" system based on pure democracy.

The United States was not designed to be a country governed by the rule of man, but one established to follow the "Laws of Nature and of Nature's God" (rule of law). Contrary to the beliefs of the liberal left progressives, the rule of law is not supposed to be based on the interpretation (opinions) of a bunch of judges, but upon authorities granted by the U.S. Constitution, which is the supreme law of the land. We the People are free to demand that their government act in a certain way. To achieve restoration of the Constitution, as we would expect from government, we are also supposed to follow the processes set forth by the Constitution during our task of keeping the republic.

A peaceful revolution can be achieved only partially by the people voting. Our peaceful revolution must also include peaceably assembling (i.e. The TEA Party, Clubs, rallies, conventions, advocacy), and engaging in the processes of civics so as to bring the whole thing to a tipping point where Washington has no choice but to listen.

A peaceful revolution is waged when the people refuse to be complacent, become informed and educated, and use their God-given talents to begin the process of taking back this country. The process of keeping the republic includes holding office, writing emails, phoning our representatives, passing out flyers, attending (or teaching, in my case) Constitution Classes, becoming active members of local patriot groups, and a whole lot of prayer.

A peaceful revolution can have an impact. It is my belief that the landslide win for conservatives in the 2010 mid-term election, 2014 mid-term election, and the election of Donald J. Trump in 2016 were directly influenced by the emergence of a peaceful patriot revolution. Our work, however, is far from finished. The revolution must continue.

The American Revolution began in meeting halls, churches, and pubs. The revolution never truly ended, however. The forces of tyranny continue to seek the destruction of liberty. They are like the current of a raging river under a boat. Like the current, the anti-constitution contingent will never stop, never rest, and never show mercy. Our revolution is one we can never truly completely win, but one we must never lose. Ours is a war of eternal vigilance that we must always fight, and one we must hand over to the next generation so that they, also, may continue the revolution to retain the Blessings of Liberty handed down to us from previous generations.

• Solution #2: Nullification

In his original draft of the Kentucky Resolutions, Thomas Jefferson wrote that "[T]he several states who formed that instrument [the Constitution], being sovereign and independent, have the unquestionable right to judge of its infraction; and that a nullification, by those [states], of all unauthorized acts….is the rightful remedy."

> **James Madison, The Father of the U.S. Constitution, encouraged the States to register their opposition to the Alien and Sedition Acts as beyond the powers given to Congress in his Virginia Resolution written in 1798. The Kentucky Resolutions of 1799, authored by Thomas Jefferson, went further than Madison's Virginia Resolution and asserted that States possessed the power to nullify unconstitutional federal laws.**

A strong central government was seen as a necessary evil. When the U.S. Constitution was written, the idea was to create a strong central government restrained by various mechanisms and checks that existed both internally (separation of powers), and externally (The States, and the people's, ability to vote into the system representatives). James Madison recognized the necessity of government as a necessary evil, understanding that human nature's tendency towards sin and a lust for power were to serve as the greatest obstacles to maintaining a system of liberty. Madison wrote in Federalist #51, "Ambition must be made to counteract ambition. The interest of the man must be connected with the constitutional rights of the place. It may be a reflection on human nature, that such devices should be necessary to control the abuses of government. But what is government itself, but the greatest of all reflections on human nature? If men were angels, no government would be necessary. If angels were to govern men, neither external nor internal controls on government would be necessary. In framing a government which is to be administered by men over men, the great difficulty lies in this: you must first enable the government to control the governed; and in the next place oblige it to control itself. A dependence on the people is, no doubt, the primary control on the government; but experience has taught mankind the necessity of auxiliary precautions."

The United States Constitution is a social contract entered into by the States and We the People. The federal government was not a party of the contract. It was a creation of the contract, established to serve the States and We the People so as to protect, preserve and promote the union of States, and the Blessings of Liberty.

Thomas Hobbes, 1588-1679, explained that a social contract was an agreement among persons to live together with the understanding that in their natural state, people can be cruel, greedy, and selfish.

Without a social contract in place to govern against the wickedness of human nature, people fight, rob, and oppress each other. To put into check the natural tendencies of human nature, social contracts are put into place. In a system of governance based on the social contract, people give up their freedom to steal from each other, or harm each other, in return for the safety and order of an organized society. A strong, central government was seen by Hobbes as being a necessary evil that was best for society because it imposes order and compels obedience.

> **For all have sinned, and come short of the glory of God; ~ Romans 3:23; King James Version (KJV)**

John Locke, 1632-1704, also wrote about the concept of the social contract, but added to his analysis the importance of individualism, natural law (God-given rights), and the personal ownership of property. In his writings, Locke explained that property is a natural right derived from labor, and that the individual ownership of goods is beneficial to human society. Like Hobbes, Locke recognized that humanity in our natural state are equal and independent, and that we have a natural right to defend our "life, health, liberty, and possessions." To protect our natural rights, however, Locke believed people needed to enter into a social contract in order to establish a civil society that guards against the violent and selfish tendencies of human nature.

James Madison referred to the U.S. Constitution as a social contract, whereby the citizens of the States of the new country may live together for their mutual benefit, retaining their natural rights, and limiting the new federal government to external issues, while leaving all internal issues to the States, and local governments. He wrote in Federalist #45, "The powers delegated by the proposed Constitution to the federal government are few and defined. Those which are to remain in the State governments are numerous and indefinite. The former will be exercised principally on external objects, as war, peace, negotiation, and foreign commerce; with which last the power of taxation will, for the most part, be connected. The powers reserved to the several States will extend to all the objects which, in the ordinary course of affairs, concern the lives, liberties, and properties of the people, and the internal order, improvement, and prosperity of the State. The operations of the federal government will be most extensive and important in times of war and danger; those of the State governments, in times of peace and security. As the former periods will probably bear a small proportion to the latter, the State governments will here enjoy another advantage over the federal government."

During the Constitutional Convention the delegates of the States were the *makers* of the social contract we call the United States Constitution, making the States constituents of the union, in addition to We the People. The States, in other words, are the parents of the federal government, and have as much authority to act as an agent of oversight over the federal government as does We the People. The States legally transferred some of their original powers to the federal government, but retained their sovereignty and autonomy for the purpose of continuing to practice the concept of *localism*. As the parents of the federal government, the States are also the final arbiters of the U.S. Constitution, which gives them the final say over what is, or is not, constitutional.

The federal government exists because the States allow it to, and that means the federal government serves the States at their pleasure. The Constitution grants to the federal government expressly enumerated powers, but if the federal government were to act in an unconstitutional manner, or pass unconstitutional laws, the States have at their disposal the power of *nullification*. Nullification is the ability of a State to refuse to abide by a federal mandate or law simply because it is unconstitutional. If the federal government passes any legislation that does not fall within the authorities granted by the Constitution, the States have the right to not follow the federal mandate or law.

As a social contract, the Constitution is a simple instrument when it comes to interpretation. As in the legal realm of contract law, the simple question that must be asked is, "Is the authority being claimed by the federal government listed in the Constitution as an expressed enumerated power? Either the authority is in there in plain and simple language, or it is not." If an authority the federal government claims to possess, and is attempting to enforce, is not listed as an authority to the federal government in the Constitution, the States do not need to abide by it, and have the right to nullify the federal law, or action.

Article VI. of the U.S. Constitution reads, "This Constitution, and the Laws of the United States which shall be made in Pursuance thereof; and all Treaties made, or which shall be made, under the Authority of the United States, shall be the Supreme Law of the Land; and the Judges in every State shall be bound thereby, any Thing in the Constitution or Laws of any State to the Contrary notwithstanding."

The clause is known as the Supremacy Clause. Laws made in pursuance of the Constitution, according to that clause, are the Supreme Law of the Land and States may not pass laws contrary to those Laws of the United States. However, if a law of the United States is not pursuant of the U.S. Constitution, then it is not a legal law, and based on the concept of nullification, a State has the legal authority to refuse to abide by the unconstitutional law.

Unfortunately, the Supremacy Clause can sometimes be used in an unconstitutional manner, as well, when a State decides to ignore a perfectly constitutional federal law. During the Nullification Crisis during 1832–1837, President Andrew Jackson had to deal with a confrontation by South Carolina when they deemed a tariff to be unconstitutional.

A little more than a decade later a number of States and territories in the northern portion of the Louisiana Purchase nullified the Fugitive Slave Act of 1850 that, while it was a constitutional law at the time, supported by Article IV. of the U.S. Constitution, the northern States deemed the law unjust and in response refused to return escaped slaves to their owners in The South. The crisis led to the Dred Scott decision in 1857. The case ultimately took more than ten years to be ruled upon by the United States Supreme Court. The lawsuit was originally filed by Scott in 1846 in State courts, and then he filed with the federal courts in 1853. The Court ruled in 1857 that slaves had no claim to freedom or citizenship. Since they were not citizens, they did not possess the legal standing to bring suit in a federal court. Slaves were seen by the court as being private property making Scott subject to the Fifth Amendment to the United States Constitution, with prohibits the taking of property from its owner "without due process". Therefore, the nullification of the Fugitive Slave Act of 1850 was rejected, and seen as being unconstitutional.

In more recent news, the State of California chose to nullify federal immigration laws by passing legislation making California a "Sanctuary State." Senate Bill 54 prohibits State and local law enforcement agencies, including school and security officers, from using money or staff to investigate, question, hold or arrest people for immigration violations; in essence, discouraging law enforcement officials from cooperating with federal immigration agencies.

The problem is that California's nullification of federal immigration laws is unconstitutional. Article I, Section 9 of the U.S. Constitution grants the authority to the United States Congress to make law prohibiting certain persons from migrating into the United States, making all immigration laws by the federal government constitutional.

Nullification, however, when the federal government imposes unconstitutional laws, can also be a powerful tool in combating federally sponsored tyranny against the States.

The Affordable Care Act, also known as Obamacare, was rejected by twenty-eight States (originally, twenty-six States, but two individual State lawsuits were added to the mix, later), who sued the federal government (seven separate cases were consolidated when they reached the U.S. Supreme Court). After all of the dust settled, a majority opinion by the Supreme Court upheld as being constitutional the unconstitutional federal intrusion into the private health care and health insurance industries.

Twenty-eight States sued the federal government using the federal courts populated by federal judges paid by federal monies. How did they think it was going to turn out?

If the State legislatures of those twenty-eight States had turned to the constitutional concept of nullification, and had stood arm-in-arm against the unconstitutional Affordable Care Act, it would have saved us wasted tax dollars on a federal lawsuit that was destined to be defeated. One wonders how the tables would have been turned if the States had simply nullified Obamacare.

Are the members of our State legislatures aware that they hold such power against the federal government? Do they understand what nullification even is? Do they fear it? If faced with a tyrannical enough piece of federal legislation, would they be willing to take such a stance?

Do We the People understand the nuances of nullification? And once we are educated regarding the constitutional tool, how do we make sure our State legislators are aware of the power, and are willing to pursue it?

Unfortunately, people tend to cringe when nullification is discussed, largely because of the role of nullification prior to the War Between the States. Some folks actually blame nullification for the commencement of the American Civil War, but erroneously believe it was the Southern States who championed the constitutionally supported strategy.

Nullification is only one of many tools on the tool belt of the States. If necessary, the States can do so much more, if only they are aware of their powers, and if they are willing to act upon them.

• Solution #3: Secession

Secession is defined as "the action of withdrawing formally from membership of a federation or body, especially a political state." The union of States called the United States of America is a voluntary union, and the States have a right to secede if they deem it necessary. Secession, or the threat of secession, often leaves folks cringing with nervousness. As voluntary members of the union, the States have the right to exit from the union if the social contract they have agreed to be a member of is being breached by the federal government. Even the mere threat of secession makes the political class of Washington, D.C. nervous.

Peaceful secession was considered by the Founding Fathers to be an essential component of the federal compact. They saw the threat of secession as being an effective a way to discipline the federal government should the political class running the central government seek an unconstitutional path of statism. If membership in the Union was not considered to be voluntary, how could the compact be genuine? Voluntary membership is a key aspect of a free society. The ability to secede is a necessary part of sovereignty. If the States' membership in the Union is not voluntary, then the States are not sovereign, nor free.

Alexander Hamilton recognized the voluntary nature

of the States' membership in the Union. He proposed that the United States should be in a state of perpetual national debt, and since the States would be on the hook for their portion of that debt, they would be less likely to secede.

The liberal left recognizes that State Sovereignty and autonomy is an obstacle to their desire to further expand the powers of the central government. To establish a powerful national government, State Sovereignty must be neutralized. A part of the tactic to neutralize the authority of the States has been to beat them into submission through the courts, and to establish that the concept of secession is both unlawful, and defiant.

Alexander Hamilton was a big government *nationalist* who would have fit into today's Democrat Party quite easily. His early attacks on the sovereignty of the States led to his attempt to try to rewrite history. He argued that the States had never been sovereign in the first place. As a statist, Hamilton recognized State Sovereignty as an important check and balance against the expansion of the central government, so he dismissed the Jeffersonian concepts of strict constructionism, and knew that once State Sovereignty, and the threat of secession, was a forgotten footnote of history, the federal government could be unleashed to do whatever it wanted without the States standing in the way, or limiting its growth.

Hamilton and his allies failed to sell the idea of a leviathan government during the Constitutional Convention, and he knew he could never convince three-quarters of the States to ratify any amendment giving away their sovereignty, so he set out to manipulate the Constitution through "interpretation" and "implied law" to remold the federal government as a system of national supremacy. Through concepts like *implied powers* and *judicial review*, Hamilton's statist successors have effectively carried out his argument against a limited federal government.

Nationalism – Nationalists, during the era of the Founding Fathers, were people who believed in a political ideology involving a strong identification of a group of individuals with a political entity defined in national terms. There are various strands of nationalism. The ideology may dictate that citizenship in a state should be limited to one ethnic, cultural or identity group. Nationalism may also include the belief that the state is of primary importance, which becomes the unhealthy love of one's government, accompanied by the aggressive desire to build that governmental system to a point that it is above all else, and becomes the ultimate provider for the public good.

Secession is a valuable tool provided to the States to combat nationalism (statism), and to halt the advances of an ever-expanding federal government.

Losing a member of the Union, in the eyes of the political class in Washington D.C., would not only represent a loss of revenue, but would be perceived as an act of defiance against the central powers. The States, as sovereign, individual, autonomous entities, entered into the constitutional social contract voluntarily, and they have a right to separate themselves from that contract, if they feel it to be necessary.

Thomas Paine, in his *Rights of Man*, wrote: "The fact therefore must be that the individuals themselves, each in his own personal and sovereign right, entered into a contract with each other to produce a government: and this is the only mode in which governments have a right to arise, and the only principle on which they have a right to exist."

John C. Calhoun, representative from South Carolina and Vice President under John Quincy Adams said: "The error is in the assumption that the General Government is a party to the constitutional compact. The States formed the compact, acting as sovereign and independent communities."

John Quincy Adams also defended the right of the States to secede. In an 1839 speech he said, "The indissoluble link of union between the people of the several states of this confederated nation is, after all, not in the right, but in the heart. If the day should ever come (may Heaven avert it!) when the affections of the people of these States shall be alienated from each other; when the fraternal spirit shall give way to cold indifference, or collision of interests shall fester into hatred, the bands of political associations will not long hold together parties no longer attracted by the magnetism of conciliated interests and kindly sympathies; to part in friendship from each other, than to be held together by constraint. Then will be the time for reverting to the precedents which occurred at the formation and adoption of the Constitution, to form again a more perfect Union by dissolving that which could no longer bind, and to leave the separated parts to be reunited by the law of political gravitation to the center."

In his book, *Democracy in America*, Alexis de Tocqueville wrote, "The Union was formed by the voluntary agreement of the States; and in uniting together they have not forfeited their nationality, nor have they been reduced to the condition of one and the same people. If one of the states chooses to withdraw from the compact, it would be difficult to disprove its right of doing so, and the Federal Government would have no means of maintaining its claims directly either by force or right."

The secession of the Southern States to form the Confederate States of America led to the American Civil War in 1860. After the end of the War Between the States, liberal left statists immediately convened constitutional delegations to declare the ordinances of secession by the southern States in

1860 and 1861 "invalid." During the Reconstruction period, the military governors also altered the southern constitutions so that they denounced secession. Eliminating the right of secession was the federal government's way of clearing the path for the rise of a strong national government so that it may stride towards a constantly expanding centralization of governmental authorities under the guise of the constitutionally established federal government.

The federal courts have also participated in the effort to eliminate the right of secession. In *Texas v. White* in 1869, Supreme Court Chief Justice Salmon P. Chase wrote that, "The union between Texas and the other states was as complete, as perpetual, and as indissoluble as the union between the original states. There was no place for reconsideration or revocation, except through revolution or through consent of the States."

In harmony with Alexander Hamilton and Abraham Lincoln, Chase's opinion regarding the *Texas v. White* decision suggested that the Union predated the States and grew from a common kindred spirit during the years leading to the American War for Independence. This collectivist mentality was also supported by Supreme Court Justice Joseph Story in his famous *Commentaries on the Constitution of the United States*.

Story channeled the fourth Chief Justice of the United States, John Marshall, and Alexander

Hamilton, in his reasoning, arguing that the Constitution was framed and ratified by the people at large, not the people of the individual States. "The constitution of a confederated republic, that is, of a national republic, formed of several states, is, or at least may be, not less an irrevocable form of government, than the constitution of a state formed and ratified by the aggregate of the several counties of the state." In his argument Story reduced the States to the status of a province, or a county.

Story defended his position with the "Supremacy Clause" in Article VI. Story contended that correspondence sent by the Philadelphia Convention accompanying the Constitution to the State ratifying conventions was aimed at a "consolidation of the Union," arguing that the Union's existence was a collective endeavor, and one that could not be dissolved.

Supporters of the concept that secession is illegal consider it to be a traitorous act by the States. Such an argument supports the idea that the United States is a nationalistic collective, rather than a voluntary union of States in a constitutional republic.

Constitutional originalists maintain that secession remains an important constitutional solution to combat tyranny with. Even in our modern political environment, secession, or the threat, thereof, may be used to stave off federal statism, and preserve constitutional principles and State Sovereignty.

Without the power to secede, the States cannot possibly be free, or sovereign members of a voluntary union. The idea that the States have no right to secede is in direct opposition to the viewpoint originally intended by the authors of the United States Constitution.

• Solution #4: Convention

The sovereignty of the States, and the individualism of the citizens, represent the greatest threats against the power that has been amassed by the ruling class that inhabits the halls of government in the United States. Over the last two centuries the enemies of the United States Constitution have been amassing power as they have worked to neutralize individuality and the autonomy of the States. We fight a war that pits collectivism against individuality, and we have been programmed systematically to reject the sovereignty of the States, or of the individual, whenever we encounter it. We have been convinced that the powers behind the federal government, and the corporatism that engages in political mercantilism, are too powerful to overcome, and that any attempt we may make to dissolve their iron fist over our lives is both foolish, and dangerous.

The United States Constitution may only be changed through the process of amendment, as established in Article V. of the U.S. Constitution. The ability to amend the Constitution was created for the primary purpose of granting additional authorities to the federal government, or taking away powers. As the parents over the federal government, the States have the final say regarding whether or not an authority may be added, or removed, by virtue of the ratification process. No matter how an amendment is proposed, in order to become a part of the Constitution, and become the law of the land, every amendment must receive at least three-quarters approval by the States.

Article V. of the Constitution establishes that amendments may be proposed either by Congress, or the States. The authority for the States to amend the United States Constitution by proposing amendments through convention was viewed by the Founding Fathers as being a way for the States to take back control of a tyrannical federal government. As the parents of the federal government, amending the Constitution through an Article V. Convention was a specifically designed mechanism for the States to grab a hold of the reins of a tyrannical federal government so that the States may reel the expanding system back into the control and oversight of the two constituencies – the States, and We the People. In an Article V. Convention the States may propose amendments, which then can be, in turn, presented to the States for approval through a three-quarters ratification vote. The Article V. Convention was not designed to, and may not be used for, rewriting the U.S. Constitution, or replacing it with a different document.

While I am not a big fan of Alexander Hamilton, Hamilton wrote a brilliant essay on the importance of the Article V. Convention in Federalist Paper #85. He wished to make the Anti-Federalists realize that despite their fears regarding the creation of a centralized federal government through the U.S. Constitution, they had a fail-safe in place that they could use in case the government began to overstep the powers granted to it by the States.

The only way to change the Constitution is through an amendment process. Throughout American History we have only seen amendments proposed by the United States Congress. To date, the States have not taken advantage of their authority to propose amendments.

Originally, during the debates in Philadelphia inside the walls of Independence Hall, the delegates of the Constitutional Convention in 1787 were determined to only allow the States to propose amendments. A majority of the delegates argued that they did not believe that allowing the Congress to propose amendments was a good idea. However, after a number of delegates argued in favor of also allowing the Congress to propose amendments, reluctantly the Founding Fathers decided to also allow the Congress to propose amendments.

An Article V. Convention, according to the language offered in the Constitution, shall be called when two-thirds of the States make an application for a convention. Their applications never expire, unless an expiration date is established in the application. Over the last two centuries, all 50 of the 50 States have applied, with over 750 applications (one State has rescinded its only application, so the current count sits at 49 States). The only involvement by the federal government is for Congress to "call" a convention when enough applications have been made, and if it so desires, to establish the style of ratification.

To "call" a convention is to set up the place and time. To date, Congress has unconstitutionally refused to call a convention.

If Congress chooses to establish the style of ratification, either by vote of the State Legislatures, or by State Conventions, it must be established at the time of calling the convention. If no style of ratification is established by Congress, the choice devolves to the States.

The purveyors of a strong central government fear convention. An Article V. Convention enables the States to team up against the federal government, proposing and ratifying amendments without federal control or influence. This means that amendments could be passed to further limit the authorities of the federal government, or clarify constitutional applications the federal government has been misinterpreting, such as the Commerce Clause and the General Welfare Clause.

Passing amendments to limit the authorities of the federal government as a whole, a particular branch of the federal government, or a smaller component of the federal government, is nothing new. The

Eleventh Amendment, for example, was proposed and ratified with the express purpose of limiting the powers of the federal court system, eliminating a portion of the range of cases the federal courts were authorized to hear.

During the entire history of the United States we have seen the statists among our political leaders discard any willingness to follow the Constitution's original intent. Instead, the statists depend on case law and judicial interpretations (and interpretations by political figures) so as to stray our society from the original intent of the Constitution, and instead follow the statist aspirations of tyrants. They have abandoned the Rule of Law and now pursue the Rule of Man.

"In questions of power, then, let no more be heard of confidence in man, but bind him down from mischief by the chains of the Constitution." ~ Thomas Jefferson

"It is hardly too strong to say that the Constitution was made to guard the people against the dangers of good intentions. There are men in all ages that mean to govern well, but they mean to govern. They promise to be good masters, but they mean to be masters." ~ Daniel Webster

Opponents of an Article V. Convention call it a "Con-Con," which is an inaccurate term. "Con-Con" stands for "Constitutional Convention." There has been only one Constitutional Convention, and that was in 1787. There should not be another "con-con." An Article V. Convention is not a con-con. An Article V. Convention is a valuable tool given to us by the framers of the Constitution as a legitimate way to restore the republic, and get a corrupt government headed for tyranny under control.

Those who challenge the safety of holding an Article V. Convention state that in today's political environment, the risk of a runaway convention is too great, so despite being given to us by the Founding Fathers on the pages of the United States Constitution, an Article V. Convention is just too risky to pursue, and therefore must not be put into play.

Alexander Hamilton argued in Federalist #85 that the fail-safe against a runaway convention is the fact that an Article V. Convention is only for the purpose of proposing amendments. Once those amendments are proposed, they still require a three-quarters ratification vote by the State legislatures (or individual State conventions). An Article V. Convention is a way for We the People, through our States, to amend the Constitution without the politicians of the federal government being involved.

If one argues against the States taking advantage of an Article V. Convention, what we are left with is Congress proposing amendments. Is that what we prefer? Should we support only allowing Congress to propose amendments without our involvement?

I recognize the concerns that many people have about an Article V. Convention, and the fear of a runaway convention should such a strategy be undertaken. In fact, I welcome those fears. As I recently told a friend who is a chapter leader of the John Birch Society, "Thank God you guys are so against an Article V. Convention. That way, if one winds up being held, I have no doubt the forces who fear such a convention would be all over it to make sure it is not influenced by non-constitutional forces, thus, ensuring that it does not become a runaway convention."

That said, there is a third kind of convention. The third kind of convention, which could lead to an Article V. Convention, or assist in convincing the States to use the tool of nullification, is a grass roots effort that audits the federal government, exposing the unconstitutional aspects of the federal government, and then making these constitutional shortcomings of the federal government aware to the State governments. In short, the concept uses constitutional literacy and public pressure on the local politicians to go after the federal politicians and their unconstitutional activities at the federal level. The concept, coined as being a "Republic Review" by G.R. Mobley (author of the We the People series of books), uses the sovereignty of We the People, and the sovereignty of the States, together in a combined effort in order to gain control of the federal government; with the possibility of the tactic also opening the door to nullification, or an Article V. Convention.

• Solution #5: Education

James Madison wrote, "A well-instructed people alone can be permanently a free people."

Thomas Jefferson offered, "Say...whether peace is best preserved by giving energy to the government, or information to the people. This last is the most certain and the most legitimate engine of government. Educate and inform the whole mass of the people. Enable them to see that it is their interest to preserve peace and order, and they will preserve them. And it requires no very high degree of education to convince them of this. They are the only sure reliance for the preservation of our liberty."

Benjamin Franklin was an optimist, but he also recognized that the Constitution was not perfect because of the basic flaws of human nature. His final assessment of the Constitution recognized his optimism, and his fears. He said, "...when you assemble a number of men to have the advantage of their joint wisdom, you inevitably assemble with those men, all their prejudices, their passions, their errors of opinion, their local interests, and their selfish views." While he was satisfied that the U.S. Constitution was a better alternative to what he expected may emerge, he understood that no constitution written could be a perfect construct.

The U.S. Constitution provides for us means by

which we may use a peaceful revolution, nullification, an Article V. Convention, and the threat of secession as a way to challenge a tyrannical system of governance should such a leviathan emerge. However, those tools cannot be utilized if the public "doesn't know what it doesn't know." Hence, the importance of spreading constitutional literacy through various educational strategies.

One wonders how history would be different if the citizens recognized that the rise of a tyranny was upon them, and then they took action to ward off such a system of bondage.

While we wish to ensure the younger generations are properly instructed, how can we instruct them if we don't understand the original intent of the U.S. Constitution ourselves?

Our own education may be accomplished through reading materials which inform us accurately the original intent of the Founding Fathers when it comes to the United States Constitution. Various publications by yours truly, Douglas V. Gibbs, such as "25 Myths of the United States Constitution," "The Basic Constitution: An Examination of the Principles and Philosophies of the United States Constitution," and "Concepts of the United States Constitution" provide a great start in our education about the original intent of the United States Constitution; as does "Hamilton's Curse" by Thomas J. DiLorenzo and "Liberty Inherited" by John L.

Hancock.

Education can be achieved through classes, reading, or media presentations. Through efforts I am engaged in we are attempting to insert Constitution Classes in the inner-cities, establish after-school programs at public schools, Civics and Constitution Studies programs at private schools, through home school study programs, and at private colleges. Constitutional literacy is being spread via radio programming, video and audio materials, and any other means we can establish.

Among my allies is the Constitution Association, a 501(c)3 non-profit organization. Learn more, or donate, at www.constitutionassociation.com.

For a complete list of publications by Douglas V. Gibbs, and upcoming titles, a list is provided on the last page of this book.

DOUGLAS V. GIBBS

• Declaration of Independence

IN CONGRESS, July 4, 1776.

The unanimous Declaration of the thirteen united States of America,

When in the Course of human events, it becomes necessary for one people to dissolve the political bands which have connected them with another, and to assume among the powers of the earth, the separate and equal station to which the Laws of Nature and of Nature's God entitle them, a decent respect to the opinions of mankind requires that they should declare the causes which impel them to the separation.

We hold these truths to be self-evident, that all men are created equal, that they are endowed by their Creator with certain unalienable Rights, that among these are Life, Liberty and the pursuit of Happiness.--That to secure these rights, Governments are instituted among Men, deriving their just powers from the consent of the governed, --That whenever any Form of Government becomes destructive of these ends, it is the Right of the People to alter or to abolish it, and to institute new Government, laying its foundation on such principles and organizing its powers in such form, as to them shall seem most likely to effect their Safety and Happiness. Prudence, indeed, will dictate that Governments long established should not be changed for light and transient causes; and accordingly all experience hath shewn, that mankind are more disposed to suffer, while evils are sufferable, than to right themselves by abolishing the forms to which they are accustomed. But when a long train of abuses and usurpations, pursuing invariably the same Object evinces a design to reduce them under absolute Despotism, it is their right, it is their duty, to throw off such Government, and to provide new Guards for their future security.--Such has been the patient sufferance of these Colonies; and such is now the necessity which constrains them to alter their former Systems of Government. The history of the present King of Great Britain is a history of repeated injuries and usurpations, all having in direct object the establishment of an absolute Tyranny over these States. To prove this, let Facts be submitted to a candid world.

He has refused his Assent to Laws, the most wholesome and necessary for the public good.

He has forbidden his Governors to pass Laws of immediate and pressing importance, unless suspended in their operation till his Assent should be obtained; and when so suspended, he has utterly neglected to attend to them.

He has refused to pass other Laws for the accommodation of large districts of people, unless those people would relinquish the right of Representation in the Legislature, a right inestimable to them and formidable to tyrants only.

He has called together legislative bodies at

places unusual, uncomfortable, and distant from the depository of their public Records, for the sole purpose of fatiguing them into compliance with his measures.

He has dissolved Representative Houses repeatedly, for opposing with manly firmness his invasions on the rights of the people.

He has refused for a long time, after such dissolutions, to cause others to be elected; whereby the Legislative powers, incapable of Annihilation, have returned to the People at large for their exercise; the State remaining in the mean time exposed to all the dangers of invasion from without, and convulsions within.

He has endeavoured to prevent the population of these States; for that purpose obstructing the Laws for Naturalization of Foreigners; refusing to pass others to encourage their migrations hither, and raising the conditions of new Appropriations of Lands.

He has obstructed the Administration of Justice, by refusing his Assent to Laws for establishing Judiciary powers.

He has made Judges dependent on his Will alone, for the tenure of their offices, and the amount and payment of their salaries.

He has erected a multitude of New Offices, and sent hither swarms of Officers to harrass our people, and eat out their substance.

He has kept among us, in times of peace, Standing Armies without the Consent of our legislatures.

He has affected to render the Military independent of and superior to the Civil power.

He has combined with others to subject us to a jurisdiction foreign to our constitution, and unacknowledged by our laws; giving his Assent to their Acts of pretended Legislation:

For Quartering large bodies of armed troops among us:

For protecting them, by a mock Trial, from punishment for any Murders which they should commit on the Inhabitants of these States:

For cutting off our Trade with all parts of the world:

For imposing Taxes on us without our Consent:

For depriving us in many cases, of the benefits of Trial by Jury:

For transporting us beyond Seas to be tried for pretended offences

For abolishing the free System of English Laws in a neighbouring Province, establishing therein an Arbitrary government, and enlarging its Boundaries so as to render it at once an example and fit instrument for introducing the same absolute rule into these Colonies:

For taking away our Charters, abolishing our most valuable Laws, and altering fundamentally the Forms of our Governments:

For suspending our own Legislatures, and declaring themselves invested with power to legislate for us in all cases whatsoever.

He has abdicated Government here, by declaring us out of his Protection and waging War against us.

He has plundered our seas, ravaged our Coasts, burnt our towns, and destroyed the lives of our people.

He is at this time transporting large Armies of foreign Mercenaries to compleat the works of death, desolation and tyranny, already begun with circumstances of Cruelty & perfidy scarcely paralleled in the most barbarous ages, and totally unworthy the Head of a civilized nation.

He has constrained our fellow Citizens taken Captive on the high Seas to bear Arms against their Country, to become the executioners of their friends and Brethren, or to fall themselves by their Hands.

He has excited domestic insurrections amongst us, and has endeavoured to bring on the inhabitants of our frontiers, the merciless Indian Savages, whose known rule of warfare, is an undistinguished destruction of all ages, sexes and conditions.

In every stage of these Oppressions We have Petitioned for Redress in the most humble terms: Our repeated Petitions have been answered only by repeated injury. A Prince whose character is thus marked by every act which may define a Tyrant, is unfit to be the ruler of a free people.

Nor have We been wanting in attentions to our Brittish brethren. We have warned them from time to time of attempts by their legislature to extend an unwarrantable jurisdiction over us. We have reminded them of the circumstances of our emigration and settlement here. We have appealed to their native justice and magnanimity, and we have conjured them by the ties of our common kindred to disavow these usurpations, which, would inevitably interrupt our connections and correspondence. They too have been deaf to the voice of justice and of consanguinity. We must, therefore, acquiesce in the necessity, which denounces our Separation, and hold them, as we hold the rest of mankind, Enemies in War, in Peace Friends.

We, therefore, the Representatives of the united States of America, in General Congress, Assembled, appealing to the Supreme Judge of the world for the rectitude of our intentions, do, in the Name, and by Authority of the good People of these Colonies, solemnly publish and declare, That these United Colonies are, and of Right ought to be Free and Independent States; that they are Absolved from all Allegiance to the British Crown, and that all political connection between them and the State of Great Britain, is and ought to be totally dissolved; and that as Free and Independent States, they have full Power to levy War, conclude Peace, contract Alliances, establish Commerce, and to do all other Acts and Things which Independent States may of right do. And for the support of this Declaration, with a firm reliance on the protection of divine Providence, we mutually pledge to each other our Lives, our Fortunes and our sacred Honor.

The 56 signatures on the Declaration appear in the positions indicated:

Column 1
Georgia:
  Button Gwinnett
  Lyman Hall
  George Walton

Column 2
North Carolina:
  William Hooper
  Joseph Hewes
  John Penn
South Carolina:
  Edward Rutledge
  Thomas Heyward, Jr.
  Thomas Lynch, Jr.
  Arthur Middleton

Column 3
Massachusetts:
  John Hancock
Maryland:
  Samuel Chase
  William Paca
  Thomas Stone
  Charles Carroll of Carrollton
Virginia:
  George Wythe
  Richard Henry Lee
  Thomas Jefferson
  Benjamin Harrison
  Thomas Nelson, Jr.

Francis Lightfoot Lee
Carter Braxton

Column 4
Pennsylvania:
Robert Morris
Benjamin Rush
Benjamin Franklin
John Morton
George Clymer
James Smith
George Taylor
James Wilson
George Ross
Delaware:
Caesar Rodney
George Read
Thomas McKean

Column 5
New York:
William Floyd
Philip Livingston
Francis Lewis
Lewis Morris
New Jersey:
Richard Stockton
John Witherspoon
Francis Hopkinson
John Hart
Abraham Clark

Column 6

New Hampshire:
  Josiah Bartlett
  William Whipple

Massachusetts:
  Samuel Adams
  John Adams
  Robert Treat Paine
  Elbridge Gerry

Rhode Island:
  Stephen Hopkins
  William Ellery

Connecticut:
  Roger Sherman
  Samuel Huntington
  William Williams
  Oliver Wolcott

New Hampshire:
  Matthew Thornton

DOUGLAS V. GIBBS

• United States Constitution

Changed or obsolete passages are in [brackets]

Preamble

We the People of the United States, in Order to form a more perfect Union, establish Justice, insure domestic Tranquility, provide for the common defence, promote the general Welfare, and secure the Blessings of Liberty to ourselves and our Posterity, do ordain and establish this Constitution for the United States of America.

Article I

Section 1

All legislative Powers herein granted shall be vested in a Congress of the United States, which shall consist of a Senate and House of Representatives.

Section 2

The House of Representatives shall be composed of Members chosen every second Year by the People of the several States, and the Electors in each State shall have the Qualifications requisite for Electors of the most numerous Branch of the State Legislature.

No Person shall be a Representative who shall not have attained to the Age of twenty five Years, and been seven Years a Citizen of the United States, and who shall not, when elected, be an Inhabitant of that State in which he shall be chosen.

[Representatives and direct Taxes shall be apportioned among the several States which may be included within this Union, according to their respective Numbers, which shall be determined by adding to the whole Number of free Persons, including those bound to Service for a Term of Years, and excluding Indians not taxed, three fifths of all other Persons.] *(Changed by section 2 of the Fourteenth Amendment)* The actual Enumeration shall be made within three Years after the first Meeting of the Congress of the United States, and within every subsequent Term of ten Years, in such Manner as they shall by Law direct. The Number of Representatives shall not exceed one for every thirty Thousand, but each State shall have at Least one Representative; and until such enumeration shall be made, the State of New Hampshire shall be entitled to chuse three, Massachusetts eight, Rhode-Island and Providence Plantations one, Connecticut five, New-York six, New Jersey four, Pennsylvania eight, Delaware one, Maryland six, Virginia ten, North Carolina five, South Carolina five, and Georgia three.

When vacancies happen in the Representation from any State, the Executive Authority thereof shall issue Writs of Election to fill such Vacancies.

The House of Representatives shall chuse their Speaker and other Officers; and shall have the sole Power of Impeachment.

Section 3

The Senate of the United States shall be composed of two Senators from each State, [chosen by the Legislature thereof] *(Changed by the Seventeenth Amendment)* for six Years; and each Senator shall have one Vote.

Immediately after they shall be assembled in Consequence of the first Election, they shall be divided as equally as may be into three Classes. The Seats of the Senators of the first Class shall be vacated at the Expiration of the second Year, of the second Class at the Expiration of the fourth Year, and of the third Class at the Expiration of the sixth Year, so that one third may be chosen every second Year; [and if Vacancies happen by Resignation, or otherwise, during the Recess of the Legislature of any State, the Executive thereof may make temporary Appointments until the next Meeting of the Legislature, which shall then fill such Vacancies.] *(Changed by the Seventeenth Amendment)*

No Person shall be a Senator who shall not have attained to the Age of thirty Years, and been nine Years a Citizen of the United States, and who shall not, when elected, be an Inhabitant of that State for which he shall be chosen.

The Vice President of the United States shall be President of the Senate, but shall have no Vote, unless they be equally divided.

The Senate shall chuse their other Officers, and also a President pro tempore, in the Absence of the Vice President, or when he shall exercise the Office of President of the United States.

The Senate shall have the sole Power to try all Impeachments. When sitting for that Purpose, they shall be on Oath or Affirmation. When the President of the United States is tried, the Chief Justice shall preside: And no Person shall be convicted without the Concurrence of two thirds of the Members present.

Judgment in Cases of Impeachment shall not extend further than to removal from Office, and disqualification to hold and enjoy any Office of honor, Trust or Profit under the United States: but the Party convicted shall nevertheless be liable and subject to Indictment, Trial, Judgment and Punishment, according to Law.

Section 4

The Times, Places and Manner of holding Elections for Senators and Representatives, shall be prescribed in each State by the Legislature thereof; but the

Congress may at any time by Law make or alter such Regulations, except as to the Places of chusing Senators.

The Congress shall assemble at least once in every Year, and such Meeting shall be [on the first Monday in December,] *(Changed by Section 2 of the Twentieth Amendment)* unless they shall by Law appoint a different Day.

Section 5

Each House shall be the Judge of the Elections, Returns and Qualifications of its own Members, and a Majority of each shall constitute a Quorum to do Business; but a smaller Number may adjourn from day to day, and may be authorized to compel the Attendance of absent Members, in such Manner, and under such Penalties as each House may provide.

Each House may determine the Rules of its Proceedings, punish its Members for disorderly Behaviour, and, with the Concurrence of two thirds, expel a Member.

Each House shall keep a Journal of its Proceedings, and from time to time publish the same, excepting such Parts as may in their Judgment require Secrecy; and the Yeas and Nays of the Members of either House on any question shall, at the Desire of one fifth of those Present, be entered on the Journal.

Neither House, during the Session of Congress, shall, without the Consent of the other, adjourn for more than three days, nor to any other Place than that in which the two Houses shall be sitting.

Section 6

The Senators and Representatives shall receive a Compensation for their Services, to be ascertained by Law, and paid out of the Treasury of the United States. They shall in all Cases, except Treason, Felony and Breach of the Peace, be privileged from Arrest during their Attendance at the Session of their respective Houses, and in going to and returning from the same; and for any Speech or Debate in either House, they shall not be questioned in any other Place.

No Senator or Representative shall, during the Time for which he was elected, be appointed to any civil Office under the Authority of the United States, which shall have been created, or the Emoluments whereof shall have been encreased during such time; and no Person holding any Office under the United States, shall be a Member of either House during his Continuance in Office.

Section 7

All Bills for raising Revenue shall originate in the House of Representatives; but the Senate may propose or concur with Amendments as on other

Bills.

Every Bill which shall have passed the House of Representatives and the Senate, shall, before it become a Law, be presented to the President of the United States: If he approve he shall sign it, but if not he shall return it, with his Objections to that House in which it shall have originated, who shall enter the Objections at large on their Journal, and proceed to reconsider it. If after such Reconsideration two thirds of that House shall agree to pass the Bill, it shall be sent, together with the Objections, to the other House, by which it shall likewise be reconsidered, and if approved by two thirds of that House, it shall become a Law. But in all such Cases the Votes of both Houses shall be determined by yeas and Nays, and the Names of the Persons voting for and against the Bill shall be entered on the Journal of each House respectively. If any Bill shall not be returned by the President within ten Days (Sundays excepted) after it shall have been presented to him, the Same shall be a Law, in like Manner as if he had signed it, unless the Congress by their Adjournment prevent its Return, in which Case it shall not be a Law.

Every Order, Resolution, or Vote to which the Concurrence of the Senate and House of Representatives may be necessary (except on a question of Adjournment) shall be presented to the President of the United States; and before the Same shall take Effect, shall be approved by him, or being disapproved by him, shall be repassed by two thirds of the Senate and House of Representatives, according to the Rules and Limitations prescribed in the Case of a Bill.

Section 8

The Congress shall have Power To lay and collect Taxes, Duties, Imposts and Excises, to pay the Debts and provide for the common Defence and general Welfare of the United States; but all Duties, Imposts and Excises shall be uniform throughout the United States;

To borrow Money on the credit of the United States;

To regulate Commerce with foreign Nations, and among the several States, and with the Indian Tribes;

To establish an uniform Rule of Naturalization, and uniform Laws on the subject of Bankruptcies throughout the United States;

To coin Money, regulate the Value thereof, and of foreign Coin, and fix the Standard of Weights and Measures;

To provide for the Punishment of counterfeiting the Securities and current Coin of the United States;

To establish Post Offices and post Roads;

To promote the Progress of Science and useful Arts, by securing for limited Times to Authors and Inventors the exclusive Right to their respective Writings and Discoveries;

To constitute Tribunals inferior to the supreme Court;

To define and punish Piracies and Felonies committed on the high Seas, and Offences against the Law of Nations;

To declare War, grant Letters of Marque and Reprisal, and make Rules concerning Captures on Land and Water;

To raise and support Armies, but no Appropriation of Money to that Use shall be for a longer Term than two Years;

To provide and maintain a Navy;

To make Rules for the Government and Regulation of the land and naval Forces;

To provide for calling forth the Militia to execute the Laws of the Union, suppress Insurrections and repel Invasions;

To provide for organizing, arming, and disciplining, the Militia, and for governing such Part of them as may be employed in the Service of the United States, reserving to the States respectively, the Appointment of the Officers, and the Authority of training the Militia according to the discipline prescribed by Congress;

To exercise exclusive Legislation in all Cases whatsoever, over such District (not exceeding ten Miles square) as may, by Cession of particular States, and the Acceptance of Congress, become the Seat of the Government of the United States, and to exercise like Authority over all Places purchased by the Consent of the Legislature of the State in which the Same shall be, for the Erection of Forts, Magazines, Arsenals, dock-Yards, and other needful Buildings;--And

To make all Laws which shall be necessary and proper for carrying into Execution the foregoing Powers, and all other Powers vested by this Constitution in the Government of the United States, or in any Department or Officer thereof.

Section 9

The Migration or Importation of such Persons as any of the States now existing shall think proper to admit, shall not be prohibited by the Congress prior to the Year one thousand eight hundred and eight, but a Tax or duty may be imposed on such Importation, not exceeding ten dollars for each Person.

The Privilege of the Writ of Habeas Corpus shall not be suspended, unless when in Cases of Rebellion or Invasion the public Safety may require it.

No Bill of Attainder or ex post facto Law shall be passed.

No Capitation, or other direct, Tax shall be laid, unless in Proportion to the Census or enumeration herein before directed to be taken.

No Tax or Duty shall be laid on Articles exported from any State.

No Preference shall be given by any Regulation of Commerce or Revenue to the Ports of one State over those of another; nor shall Vessels bound to, or from, one State, be obliged to enter, clear, or pay Duties in another.

No Money shall be drawn from the Treasury, but in Consequence of Appropriations made by Law; and a regular Statement and Account of the Receipts and Expenditures of all public Money shall be published from time to time.

No Title of Nobility shall be granted by the United States: And no Person holding any Office of Profit or Trust under them, shall, without the Consent of the Congress, accept of any present, Emolument, Office, or Title, of any kind whatever, from any King, Prince, or foreign State.

Section 10

No State shall enter into any Treaty, Alliance, or Confederation; grant Letters of Marque and Reprisal; coin Money; emit Bills of Credit; make any Thing but gold and silver Coin a Tender in Payment of Debts; pass any Bill of Attainder, ex post facto Law, or Law impairing the Obligation of Contracts, or grant any Title of Nobility.

No State shall, without the Consent of the Congress, lay any Imposts or Duties on Imports or Exports, except what may be absolutely necessary for executing it's inspection Laws: and the net Produce of all Duties and Imposts, laid by any State on Imports or Exports, shall be for the Use of the Treasury of the United States; and all such Laws shall be subject to the Revision and Controul of the Congress.

No State shall, without the Consent of Congress, lay any Duty of Tonnage, keep Troops, or Ships of War in time of Peace, enter into any Agreement or Compact with another State, or with a foreign Power, or engage in War, unless actually invaded, or in such imminent Danger as will not admit of delay.

Article II

Section 1

The executive Power shall be vested in a President of the United States of America. He shall hold his Office during the Term of four Years, and, together with the Vice President, chosen for the same Term, be elected, as follows:

Each State shall appoint, in such Manner as the Legislature thereof may direct, a Number of Electors, equal to the whole Number of Senators and Representatives to which the State may be entitled in the Congress: but no Senator or Representative, or Person holding an Office of Trust or Profit under the United States, shall be appointed an Elector.

[The Electors shall meet in their respective States, and vote by Ballot for two Persons, of whom one at least shall not be an Inhabitant of the same State with themselves. And they shall make a List of all the Persons voted for, and of the Number of Votes for each; which List they shall sign and certify, and transmit sealed to the Seat of the Government of the United States, directed to the President of the Senate. The President of the Senate shall, in the Presence of the Senate and House of Representatives, open all the Certificates, and the Votes shall then be counted. The Person having the greatest Number of Votes shall be the President, if such Number be a Majority of the whole Number of Electors appointed; and if there be more than one who have such Majority, and have an equal Number of Votes, then the House of Representatives shall immediately chuse by Ballot one of them for President; and if no Person have a

Majority, then from the five highest on the List the said House shall in like Manner chuse the President. But in chusing the President, the Votes shall be taken by States, the Representation from each State having one Vote; A quorum for this purpose shall consist of a Member or Members from two thirds of the States, and a Majority of all the States shall be necessary to a Choice. In every Case, after the Choice of the President, the Person having the greatest Number of Votes of the Electors shall be the Vice President. But if there should remain two or more who have equal Votes, the Senate shall chuse from them by Ballot the Vice President.] *(Changed by the Twelfth Amendment)*

The Congress may determine the Time of chusing the Electors, and the Day on which they shall give their Votes; which Day shall be the same throughout the United States.

No Person except a natural born Citizen, or a Citizen of the United States, at the time of the Adoption of this Constitution, shall be eligible to the Office of President; neither shall any Person be eligible to that Office who shall not have attained to the Age of thirty five Years, and been fourteen Years a Resident within the United States.

[In Case of the Removal of the President from Office, or of his Death, Resignation, or Inability to discharge the Powers and Duties of the said Office, the Same shall devolve on the Vice President, and the Congress may by Law provide for the Case of Removal, Death, Resignation or Inability, both of the President and Vice President, declaring what Officer shall then act as President, and such Officer shall act accordingly, until the Disability be removed, or a President shall be elected.] *(Changed by the Twenty-Fifth Amendment)*

The President shall, at stated Times, receive for his Services, a Compensation, which shall neither be increased nor diminished during the Period for which he shall have been elected, and he shall not receive within that Period any other Emolument from the United States, or any of them.

Before he enter on the Execution of his Office, he shall take the following Oath or Affirmation:--"I do solemnly swear (or affirm) that I will faithfully execute the Office of President of the United States, and will to the best of my Ability, preserve, protect and defend the Constitution of the United States."

Section 2

The President shall be Commander in Chief of the Army and Navy of the United States, and of the Militia of the several States, when called into the actual Service of the United States; he may require the Opinion, in writing, of the principal Officer in each of the executive Departments, upon any Subject relating to the Duties of their respective Offices, and he shall have Power to grant Reprieves and Pardons for Offences against the United States, except in Cases of Impeachment.

He shall have Power, by and with the Advice and Consent of the Senate, to make Treaties, provided two thirds of the Senators present concur; and he shall nominate, and by and with the Advice and Consent of the Senate, shall appoint Ambassadors, other public Ministers and Consuls, Judges of the supreme Court, and all other Officers of the United States, whose Appointments are not herein otherwise provided for, and which shall be established by Law: but the Congress may by Law vest the Appointment of such inferior Officers, as they think proper, in the President alone, in the Courts of Law, or in the Heads of Departments.

The President shall have Power to fill up all Vacancies that may happen during the Recess of the Senate, by granting Commissions which shall expire at the End of their next Session.

Section 3

He shall from time to time give to the Congress Information of the State of the Union, and recommend to their Consideration such Measures as he shall judge necessary and expedient; he may, on extraordinary Occasions, convene both Houses, or either of them, and in Case of Disagreement between them, with Respect to the Time of Adjournment, he may adjourn them to such Time as he shall think proper; he shall receive Ambassadors and other public Ministers; he shall take Care that the Laws be faithfully executed, and shall Commission all the Officers of the United States.

Section 4

The President, Vice President and all civil Officers of the United States, shall be removed from Office on Impeachment for, and Conviction of, Treason, **Bribery**, or other high Crimes and Misdemeanors.

Article III

Section 1

The judicial Power of the United States shall be vested in one supreme Court, and in such inferior Courts as the Congress may from time to time ordain and establish. The Judges, both of the supreme and inferior Courts, shall hold their Offices during good Behaviour, and shall, at stated Times, receive for their Services a Compensation, which shall not be diminished during their Continuance in Office.

Section 2

The judicial Power shall extend to all Cases, in Law and Equity, arising under this Constitution, the Laws of the United States, and Treaties made, or which shall be made, under their Authority;--to all Cases affecting Ambassadors, other public Ministers and

Consuls;--to all Cases of admiralty and maritime Jurisdiction;--to Controversies to which the United States shall be a Party;--to Controversies between two or more States;-- [between a State and Citizens of another State,] *(Changed by the Eleventh Amendment)* --between Citizens of different States,-- between Citizens of the same State claiming Lands under Grants of different States, [and between a State, or the Citizens thereof, and foreign States, Citizens or Subjects.] *(Changed by the Eleventh Amendment)*

In all Cases affecting Ambassadors, other public Ministers and Consuls, and those in which a State shall be Party, the supreme Court shall have original Jurisdiction. In all the other Cases before mentioned, the supreme Court shall have appellate Jurisdiction, both as to Law and Fact, with such Exceptions, and under such Regulations as the Congress shall make.

The Trial of all Crimes, except in Cases of Impeachment, shall be by Jury; and such Trial shall be held in the State where the said Crimes shall have been committed; but when not committed within any State, the Trial shall be at such Place or Places as the Congress may by Law have directed.

Section 3

Treason against the United States, shall consist only in levying War against them, or in adhering to their Enemies, giving them Aid and Comfort. No Person shall be convicted of Treason unless on the Testimony of two Witnesses to the same overt Act, or on Confession in open Court.

The Congress shall have Power to declare the Punishment of Treason, but no Attainder of Treason shall work Corruption of Blood, or Forfeiture except during the Life of the Person attainted.

Article IV

Section 1

Full Faith and Credit shall be given in each State to the public Acts, Records, and judicial Proceedings of every other State. And the Congress may by general Laws prescribe the Manner in which such Acts, Records and Proceedings shall be proved, and the Effect thereof.

Section 2

The Citizens of each State shall be entitled to all Privileges and Immunities of Citizens in the several States.

A Person charged in any State with Treason, Felony, or other Crime, who shall flee from Justice, and be found in another State, shall on Demand of the executive Authority of the State from which he fled, be delivered up, to be removed to the State having Jurisdiction of the Crime.

[No Person held to Service or Labour in one State, under the Laws thereof, escaping into another, shall, in Consequence of any Law or Regulation therein, be discharged from such Service or Labour, but shall be delivered up on Claim of the Party to whom such Service or Labour may be due.] *(Changed by the Thirteenth Amendment)*

Section 3

New States may be admitted by the Congress into this Union; but no new State shall be formed or erected within the Jurisdiction of any other State; nor any State be formed by the Junction of two or more States, or Parts of States, without the Consent of the Legislatures of the States concerned as well as of the Congress.

The Congress shall have Power to dispose of and make all needful Rules and Regulations respecting the Territory or other Property belonging to the United States; and nothing in this Constitution shall be so construed as to Prejudice any Claims of the United States, or of any particular State.

Section 4

The United States shall guarantee to every State in this Union a Republican Form of Government, and shall protect each of them against Invasion; and on Application of the Legislature, or of the Executive (when the Legislature cannot be convened), against domestic Violence.

Article V

The Congress, whenever two thirds of both Houses shall deem it necessary, shall propose Amendments to this Constitution, or, on the Application of the Legislatures of two thirds of the several States, shall call a Convention for proposing Amendments, which, in either Case, shall be valid to all Intents and Purposes, as Part of this Constitution, when ratified by the Legislatures of three fourths of the several States, or by Conventions in three fourths thereof, as the one or the other Mode of Ratification may be proposed by the Congress; Provided that no Amendment which may be made prior to the Year One thousand eight hundred and eight shall in any Manner affect the first and fourth Clauses in the Ninth Section of the first Article; and that no State, without its Consent, shall be deprived of its equal Suffrage in the Senate.

Article VI

All Debts contracted and Engagements entered into, before the Adoption of this Constitution, shall be as valid against the United States under this Constitution, as under the Confederation.

This Constitution, and the Laws of the United States which shall be made in Pursuance thereof; and all

Treaties made, or which shall be made, under the Authority of the United States, shall be the supreme Law of the Land; and the Judges in every State shall be bound thereby, any Thing in the Constitution or Laws of any State to the Contrary notwithstanding.

The Senators and Representatives before mentioned, and thé Members of the several State Legislatures, and all executive and judicial Officers, both of the United States and of the several States, shall be bound by Oath or Affirmation, to support this Constitution; but no religious Test shall ever be required as a Qualification to any Office or public Trust under the United States.

Article VII

The Ratification of the Conventions of nine States, shall be sufficient for the Establishment of this Constitution between the States so ratifying the Same.

done in Convention by the Unanimous Consent of the States present the Seventeenth Day of September in the Year of our Lord one thousand seven hundred and Eighty seven and of the Independance of the United States of America the Twelfth In witness whereof We have hereunto subscribed our Names,

G°. Washington
Presidt and deputy from Virginia

Delaware
Geo: Read
Gunning Bedford jun
John Dickinson
Richard Bassett
Jaco: Broom

Maryland
James McHenry
Dan of St Thos. Jenifer
Danl. Carroll

Virginia
John Blair
James Madison Jr.

North Carolina
Wm. Blount
Richd. Dobbs Spaight
Hu Williamson

South Carolina
J. Rutledge
Charles Cotesworth Pinckney
Charles Pinckney
Pierce Butler

Georgia
William Few
Abr Baldwin

New Hampshire
John Langdon
Nicholas Gilman

Massachusetts
Nathaniel Gorham
Rufus King

Connecticut
Wm. Saml. Johnson
Roger Sherman

New York
Alexander Hamilton

New Jersey
Wil: Livingston
David Brearley
Wm. Paterson
Jona: Dayton

Pennsylvania
B Franklin
Thomas Mifflin
Robt. Morris
Geo. Clymer
Thos. FitzSimons
Jared Ingersoll
James Wilson
Gouv Morris

Bill of Rights – Amendments 1-10, Ratified December 15, 1791

Amendment I

Congress shall make no law respecting an establishment of religion, or prohibiting the free exercise thereof; or abridging the freedom of speech, or of the press; or the right of the people peaceably to assemble, and to petition the Government for a redress of grievances.

Amendment II

A well regulated Militia, being necessary to the security of a free State, the right of the people to keep and bear Arms, shall not be infringed.

Amendment III

No Soldier shall, in time of peace be quartered in any house, without the consent of the Owner, nor in time of war, but in a manner to be prescribed by law.

Amendment IV

The right of the people to be secure in their persons, houses, papers, and effects, against unreasonable searches and seizures, shall not be violated, and no Warrants shall issue, but upon probable cause, supported by Oath or affirmation, and particularly describing the place to be searched, and the persons or things to be seized.

Amendment V

No person shall be held to answer for a capital, or otherwise infamous crime, unless on a presentment or indictment of a Grand Jury, except in cases arising in the land or naval forces, or in the Militia, when in actual service in time of War or public danger; nor shall any person be subject for the same offence to be twice put in jeopardy of life or limb; nor shall be compelled in any criminal case to be a witness against himself, nor be deprived of life, liberty, or property, without due process of law; nor shall private property be taken for public use, without just compensation.

Amendment VI

In all criminal prosecutions, the accused shall enjoy the right to a speedy and public trial, by an impartial jury of the State and district wherein the crime shall have been committed, which district shall have been previously ascertained by law, and to be informed of the nature and cause of the accusation; to be confronted with the witnesses against him; to have compulsory process for obtaining witnesses in his favor, and to have the Assistance of Counsel for his defence.

Amendment VII

In Suits at common law, where the value in controversy shall exceed twenty dollars, the right of trial by jury shall be preserved, and no fact tried by a jury, shall be otherwise re-examined in any Court of the United States, than according to the rules of the common law.

Amendment VIII

Excessive bail shall not be required, nor excessive fines imposed, nor cruel and unusual punishments inflicted.

Amendment IX

The enumeration in the Constitution, of certain rights, shall not be construed to deny or disparage others retained by the people.

Amendment X

The powers not delegated to the United States by the Constitution, nor prohibited by it to the States, are reserved to the States respectively, or to the people.

Amendments 11-27

Amendment XI

Passed by Congress March 4, 1794. Ratified February 7, 1795.

The Judicial power of the United States shall not be construed to extend to any suit in law or equity, commenced or prosecuted against one of the United States by Citizens of another State, or by Citizens or Subjects of any Foreign State.

Amendment XII

Passed by Congress December 9, 1803. Ratified June 15, 1804.

The Electors shall meet in their respective states and vote by ballot for President and Vice-President, one of whom, at least, shall not be an inhabitant of the same state with themselves; they shall name in their ballots the person voted for as President, and in distinct ballots the person voted for as Vice-President, and they shall make distinct lists of all persons voted for as President, and of all persons voted for as Vice-President, and of the number of votes for each, which lists they shall sign and certify, and transmit sealed to the seat of the government of the United States, directed to the President of the Senate; -- the President of the Senate shall, in the presence of the Senate and House of

Representatives, open all the certificates and the votes shall then be counted; -- The person having the greatest number of votes for President, shall be the President, if such number be a majority of the whole number of Electors appointed; and if no person have such majority, then from the persons having the highest numbers not exceeding three on the list of those voted for as President, the House of Representatives shall choose immediately, by ballot, the President. But in choosing the President, the votes shall be taken by states, the representation from each state having one vote; a quorum for this purpose shall consist of a member or members from two-thirds of the states, and a majority of all the states shall be necessary to a choice. [And if the House of Representatives shall not choose a President whenever the right of choice shall devolve upon them, before the fourth day of March next following, then the Vice-President shall act as President, as in case of the death or other constitutional disability of the President. −] *(Superseded by section 3 of the Twentieth Amendment)* The person having the greatest number of votes as Vice-President, shall be the Vice-President, if such number be a majority of the whole number of Electors appointed, and if no person have a majority, then from the two highest numbers on the list, the Senate shall choose the Vice-President; a quorum for the purpose shall consist of two-thirds of the whole number of Senators, and a majority of the whole number shall be necessary to a choice. But no person constitutionally ineligible to the office of

President shall be eligible to that of Vice-President of the United States.

Amendment XIII

Passed by Congress January 31, 1865. Ratified December 6, 1865.

Section 1.
Neither slavery nor involuntary servitude, except as a punishment for crime whereof the party shall have been duly convicted, shall exist within the United States, or any place subject to their jurisdiction.

Section 2.
Congress shall have power to enforce this article by appropriate legislation.

Amendment XIV

Passed by Congress June 13, 1866. Ratified July 9, 1868.

Section 1.
All persons born or naturalized in the United States, and subject to the jurisdiction thereof, are citizens of the United States and of the State wherein they reside. No State shall make or enforce any law which shall abridge the privileges or immunities of citizens of the United States; nor shall any State deprive any person of life, liberty, or property, without due process of law; nor deny to any person within its

jurisdiction the equal protection of the laws.

Section 2.
Representatives shall be apportioned among the several States according to their respective numbers, counting the whole number of persons in each State, excluding Indians not taxed. But when the right to vote at any election for the choice of electors for President and Vice-President of the United States, Representatives in Congress, the Executive and Judicial officers of a State, or the members of the Legislature thereof, is denied to any of the male inhabitants of such State, [being twenty-one years of age,] *(Changed by section 1 of the 26th amendment)* and citizens of the United States, or in any way abridged, except for participation in rebellion, or other crime, the basis of representation therein shall be reduced in the proportion which the number of such male citizens shall bear to the whole number of male citizens twenty-one years of age in such State.

Section 3.
No person shall be a Senator or Representative in Congress, or elector of President and Vice-President, or hold any office, civil or military, under the United States, or under any State, who, having previously taken an oath, as a member of Congress, or as an officer of the United States, or as a member of any State legislature, or as an executive or judicial officer of any State, to support the Constitution of the United States, shall have engaged in insurrection or rebellion against the same, or given aid or comfort to

the enemies thereof. But Congress may by a vote of two-thirds of each House, remove such disability.

Section 4.
The validity of the public debt of the United States, authorized by law, including debts incurred for payment of pensions and bounties for services in suppressing insurrection or rebellion, shall not be questioned. But neither the United States nor any State shall assume or pay any debt or obligation incurred in aid of insurrection or rebellion against the United States, or any claim for the loss or emancipation of any slave; but all such debts, obligations and claims shall be held illegal and void.

Section 5.
The Congress shall have the power to enforce, by appropriate legislation, the provisions of this article.

Amendment XV

Passed by Congress February 26, 1869. Ratified February 3, 1870.

Section 1.
The right of citizens of the United States to vote shall not be denied or abridged by the United States or by any State on account of race, color, or previous condition of servitude--

Section 2.
The Congress shall have the power to enforce this

article by appropriate legislation.

Amendment XVI

Passed by Congress July 2, 1909. Ratified February 3, 1913.

The Congress shall have power to lay and collect taxes on incomes, from whatever source derived, without apportionment among the several States, and without regard to any census or enumeration.

Amendment XVII

Passed by Congress May 13, 1912. Ratified April 8, 1913.

The Senate of the United States shall be composed of two Senators from each State, elected by the people thereof, for six years; and each Senator shall have one vote. The electors in each State shall have the qualifications requisite for electors of the most numerous branch of the State legislatures.

When vacancies happen in the representation of any State in the Senate, the executive authority of such State shall issue writs of election to fill such vacancies: Provided, That the legislature of any State may empower the executive thereof to make temporary appointments until the people fill the vacancies by election as the legislature may direct.

This amendment shall not be so construed as to affect the election or term of any Senator chosen before it becomes valid as part of the Constitution.

Amendment XVIII

Passed by Congress December 18, 1917. Ratified January 16, 1919.

[Section 1.
After one year from the ratification of this article the manufacture, sale, or transportation of intoxicating liquors within, the importation thereof into, or the exportation thereof from the United States and all territory subject to the jurisdiction thereof for beverage purposes is hereby prohibited.

Section 2.
The Congress and the several States shall have concurrent power to enforce this article by appropriate legislation.

Section 3.
This article shall be inoperative unless it shall have been ratified as an amendment to the Constitution by the legislatures of the several States, as provided in the Constitution, within seven years from the date of the submission hereof to the States by the Congress.]
(Repealed by amendment 21)

Amendment XIX

Passed by Congress June 4, 1919. Ratified August 18, 1920.

The right of citizens of the United States to vote shall not be denied or abridged by the United States or by any State on account of sex.

Congress shall have power to enforce this article by appropriate legislation.

Amendment XX

Passed by Congress March 2, 1932. Ratified January 23, 1933.

Section 1.
The terms of the President and the Vice President shall end at noon on the 20th day of January, and the terms of Senators and Representatives at noon on the 3rd day of January, of the years in which such terms would have ended if this article had not been ratified; and the terms of their successors shall then begin.

Section 2.
The Congress shall assemble at least once in every year, and such meeting shall begin at noon on the 3d day of January, unless they shall by law appoint a different day.

Section 3.
If, at the time fixed for the beginning of the term of the President, the President elect shall have died, the

Vice President elect shall become President. If a President shall not have been chosen before the time fixed for the beginning of his term, or if the President elect shall have failed to qualify, then the Vice President elect shall act as President until a President shall have qualified; and the Congress may by law provide for the case wherein neither a President elect nor a Vice President shall have qualified, declaring who shall then act as President, or the manner in which one who is to act shall be selected, and such person shall act accordingly until a President or Vice President shall have qualified.

Section 4.
The Congress may by law provide for the case of the death of any of the persons from whom the House of Representatives may choose a President whenever the right of choice shall have devolved upon them, and for the case of the death of any of the persons from whom the Senate may choose a Vice President whenever the right of choice shall have devolved upon them.

Section 5.
Sections 1 and 2 shall take effect on the 15th day of October following the ratification of this article.

Section 6.
This article shall be inoperative unless it shall have been ratified as an amendment to the Constitution by the legislatures of three-fourths of the several States within seven years from the date of its submission.

Amendment XXI

Passed by Congress February 20, 1933. Ratified December 5, 1933.

Section 1.
The eighteenth article of amendment to the Constitution of the United States is hereby repealed.

Section 2.
The transportation or importation into any State, Territory, or Possession of the United States for delivery or use therein of intoxicating liquors, in violation of the laws thereof, is hereby prohibited.

Section 3.
This article shall be inoperative unless it shall have been ratified as an amendment to the Constitution by conventions in the several States, as provided in the Constitution, within seven years from the date of the submission hereof to the States by the Congress.

Amendment XXII

Passed by Congress March 21, 1947. Ratified February 27, 1951.

Section 1.
No person shall be elected to the office of the President more than twice, and no person who has held the office of President, or acted as President, for

more than two years of a term to which some other person was elected President shall be elected to the office of President more than once. But this Article shall not apply to any person holding the office of President when this Article was proposed by Congress, and shall not prevent any person who may be holding the office of President, or acting as President, during the term within which this Article becomes operative from holding the office of President or acting as President during the remainder of such term.

Section 2.
This article shall be inoperative unless it shall have been ratified as an amendment to the Constitution by the legislatures of three-fourths of the several States within seven years from the date of its submission to the States by the Congress.

Amendment XXIII

Passed by Congress June 16, 1960. Ratified March 29, 1961.

Section 1.
The District constituting the seat of Government of the United States shall appoint in such manner as Congress may direct:

A number of electors of President and Vice President equal to the whole number of Senators and Representatives in Congress to which the District would be entitled if it were a State, but in no event more than the least populous State; they shall be in addition to those appointed by the States, but they shall be considered, for the purposes of the election of President and Vice President, to be electors appointed by a State; and they shall meet in the District and perform such duties as provided by the twelfth article of amendment.

Section 2.
The Congress shall have power to enforce this article by appropriate legislation.
Amendment XXIV

Passed by Congress August 27, 1962. Ratified January 23, 1964.

Section 1.
The right of citizens of the United States to vote in any primary or other election for President or Vice President, for electors for President or Vice President, or for Senator or Representative in Congress, shall not be denied or abridged by the United States or any State by reason of failure to pay poll tax or other tax.

Section 2.
The Congress shall have power to enforce this article by appropriate legislation.

Amendment XXV

Passed by Congress July 6, 1965. Ratified February 10, 1967.

Section 1.
In case of the removal of the President from office or of his death or resignation, the Vice President shall become President.

Section 2.
Whenever there is a vacancy in the office of the Vice President, the President shall nominate a Vice President who shall take office upon confirmation by a majority vote of both Houses of Congress.

Section 3.
Whenever the President transmits to the President pro tempore of the Senate and the Speaker of the House of Representatives his written declaration that he is unable to discharge the powers and duties of his office, and until he transmits to them a written declaration to the contrary, such powers and duties shall be discharged by the Vice President as Acting President.

Section 4.
Whenever the Vice President and a majority of either the principal officers of the executive departments or of such other body as Congress may by law provide, transmit to the President pro tempore of the Senate and the Speaker of the House of Representatives their written declaration that the President is unable to discharge the powers and duties of his office, the

Vice President shall immediately assume the powers and duties of the office as Acting President.

Thereafter, when the President transmits to the President pro tempore of the Senate and the Speaker of the House of Representatives his written declaration that no inability exists, he shall resume the powers and duties of his office unless the Vice President and a majority of either the principal officers of the executive department or of such other body as Congress may by law provide, transmit within four days to the President pro tempore of the Senate and the Speaker of the House of Representatives their written declaration that the President is unable to discharge the powers and duties of his office. Thereupon Congress shall decide the issue, assembling within forty-eight hours for that purpose if not in session. If the Congress, within twenty-one days after receipt of the latter written declaration, or, if Congress is not in session, within twenty-one days after Congress is required to assemble, determines by two-thirds vote of both Houses that the President is unable to discharge the powers and duties of his office, the Vice President shall continue to discharge the same as Acting President; otherwise, the President shall resume the powers and duties of his office.

Amendment XXVI

Passed by Congress March 23, 1971. Ratified July 1, 1971.

Section 1.
The right of citizens of the United States, who are eighteen years of age or older, to vote shall not be denied or abridged by the United States or by any State on account of age.

Section 2.
The Congress shall have power to enforce this article by appropriate legislation.

Amendment XXVII

Originally proposed Sept. 25, 1789. Ratified May 7, 1992.

No law, varying the compensation for the services of the Senators and Representatives, shall take effect, until an election of representatives shall have intervened.

Note: Congress submitted the text of the Twenty-Seventh Amendment to the States as part of the proposed Bill of Rights on September 25, 1789. The Amendment was not ratified together with the first Ten Amendments, which became effective on December 15, 1791. The Twenty-Seventh Amendment was ratified on May 7, 1992, by the vote of Michigan.

TITLES BY DOUGLAS V. GIBBS

25 Myths of the United States Constitution

The Basic Constitution: An Examination of the Principles and Philosophies of the United States Constitution

Concepts of the United States Constitution

Silenced Screams: Abortion in a Virtuous Society

COMING SOON BY DOUGLAS V. GIBBS

(Dates of release are estimated)

4th Quarter 2017: 7 Worst Constitutional Liars
1st Quarter 2018: A Promise of American Liberty
3rd Quarter 2018: A Tyrant's Guide to Killing Liberty
4th Quarter 2018: Across the Gray Line – Ideologies Contrasted
1st Quarter 2019: A Promise of Economic Freedom
2nd Quarter 2019: John Marshall and Nine Rulings That Changed the Constitution
3rd Quarter 2019: 50 Greatest Influences on the U.S. Constitution
4th Quarter 2019: Elizabeth Powel, Keeper of the Republic
2nd Quarter 2020: A Patriot's Guide to the United States Constitution
3rd Quarter 2020: Timeline of Liberty
1st Quarter 2021: Madison's Notes – Understanding the Debates of the Constitutional Convention

Made in the USA
Middletown, DE
24 June 2021